CASH FIRE
By Caroline Fielding

Picture this. You are home on a Sunday thinking about how much overtime you have to work next week to pay your electric bill, or perhaps you are thinking about how to afford that cruise vacation you were invited on with a group of high school friends next summer. You need extra money; however, you do not know the first thing about starting a business. You do not have any clue about how corporations, LLC's, or sole proprietorships work. You do not even have the money to start up an actual, legitimate, business. Perhaps you already have a part time or full time job and you have no extra time to devote to an extra "real" job with zero flexibility and set hours. You have researched the internet for ideas but have no inclination to try what thousands of others are trying: creating a blog or website. Even if you did have the inclination, you do not know how to gain advertisers to sustain the sites. You are not a good writer or communicator, you do not want the hassle of employees, board of directors, or payroll accounts. The banks are hardly shelling out any money these days and your credit is not so great anyway. You just simply want extra cash. More importantly, you simply want to make extra cash quickly. How do you accomplish this? Where do I even start? "I have no good ideas," you tell yourself! What can I do right now, to begin to make some extra cash that doesn't involve a great big hassle, or a huge amount of money? No need to wonder anymore, I will give you some suggestions and creative ideas in this book. Some of these ideas are more sustainable than others, some require more time, some require less time, but I sincerely hope one of these innovative ideas bring a little bit of hope and of course, extra cash, to your doorstep in no time!

*RESEARCH BULK PICK UP DAY

Search online or make a phone call to your county's or city's solid waste department to find out the dates of their bulk pick up day. This is usually once or twice per year. People throw out the strangest and coolest items. Coffee tables, dresser drawers, old televisions, grills, pictures, and more, are often left on the side of the road on bulk pick up day. People do not have the time or desire to take items to the dump, clean them up, gather them for the local thrift shop or host a garage sale. Take advantage of this! Most people agree it is much easier to bring unwanted items to the curb , turn around, go back inside, and be done with them! This is your opportunity! Drive around with your car, or borrow a pick-up truck, and take items that are easy enough to be cleaned or cheaply painted or re-stained, fix them up, and post those items on Craig's List, eBay, rent a cheap booth at a flea market, or host your own garage sale. These are completely free items don't forget. This is all profit. Just a little sweat equity in cleaning up the items, hammering a few nails in a coffee table leg that is falling off, putting a little carpenter's glue on an item to secure it, or cleaning up a painting, can leave the item looking in pretty good shape. Just think, if you pick up one coffee table, one bedroom dresser, an old grill, and a television stand, and sell each item for just $10, you have just made $40 bucks. Just like that. Ten dollars is cheap too, just think if you prepare the items to be in better shape, and then sold them each for $50 each. That is $200 right there. Easy, quick cash! If you make several trips back and forth from the neighborhood to your home, and drop off several loads, you can spend the next month or so fixing them up, host a garage sale, then have a nice stack of cash to your name. Every city and county has bulk pick up days at least once per year, but many have it twice per year, or even quarterly. So, remember to call ahead and put this on your calendar.

It is amazing what a little cheap 99 cent can of spray paint and cleaning will do to fishing poles, hockey sticks, helmets, sporting equipment, flower pots, and other household items, as well as furniture. Use your imagination and get creative to turn items into decorative furniture. Turn a small china cabinet into a jewelry armoire. Turn a coffee table into a pub table by just adding some longer legs you can find at any hardware store. Clean up old glass jars, add paint with stencils and create a Q-tip holder or cotton ball holder for a bathroom. Creative minds will love this idea and will probably have a hard time parting with the creations that they come up with. Crafty websites and DIY project ideas are very prevalent all over the internet, so if you find an item that you are not quite sure what to do with, research the item and surely you will see a ton of great ideas for it.

*SEARCH YOUR ATTIC/SEARCH ESTATE SALES

Books, collectables, baseball cards, coins, and tools are all items that can be re-sold at a decent profit. Think of this as an attic-flip. If you have an attic full of this type of stuff, take a look and search the internet to see what items are worth. Then start digging. This may take a full few days, but the time that you put into this project is worth it, especially if you find items that are attractive to collectors. Scour the internet auction and antique websites to find out which items sell and go hunt for those items at garage sales and estate sales. Become knowledgeable about prices and, over time, you will be able to spot a good collection-flip right away.

If you are lucky enough to have collectibles in your attic, or perhaps you inherited old boxes from a family member, it is best to make an inventory of what you have with a spreadsheet software, or write down the items in a spiral notebook (keeping it simple is sometimes much better). Next to the item description, research the price range on auction/collector sites on the internet, then put the range next to that item. This way, you can organize the items by price and by alphabetical order. If you charge 10% less, you are sure to have quick sales. However, with this endeavor, definitely do your homework. You want to make absolutely sure you are not selling a $3 baseball card when it is actually worth $1,000,000. Boy, that would ruin your day.

*WHAT CAN YOU DO FOR A $5 OR $10 ADMISSION CHARGE

Think about what your knowledge is, or what you are good at, and think about hosting a night or weekend day at your house or a free public area to teach others, (such as a park or a public beach) and charge $10 admission. I will give you some examples here.

Dance. If you are good at yoga, hip hop dance, salsa dancing, etc., offer a 4 week course for $10 on a weekend day or weekday evening. Bring a boombox or speaker system and you are all set. Start from the basic steps and progress into the advanced steps. You will have a blast seeing the worst dancer become your best, at the end of the course. That will be just as satisfying as the cash you now have!

Fitness. You have no rhythm and zero dance skills? Do you consider yourself more of an athletic type? If you are a runner, a biker, a weight trainer, or know how to set up an obstacle course boot camp, then do this! Form a run club where everyone pays $5 per week, and initiate runs 3 evenings a week together. Print out a roster of runners with names and email addresses or phone numbers, and a print out a blank log where the runners can track their miles, times and compare notes. This builds a sense of camaraderie. Give every runner a list of the other runners' phone numbers and contact information (with their permission of course). This way, the runners are more apt to form relationships and keep coming back week after week, meaning you keep getting $5 per week from every runner, and hopefully expanding your club. You can do this for biking also. Form a bike group, map out some trails in a neighborhood, or off-road for a change of scenery, and form the same type of group. Do this for weight training as well. If you have weights, bring them to a city park, charge interested people $5 for 2 weeks and teach them proper ways to weight train, proper ways to pick up and lift weights, etc. Grab some old tires, ropes, a rope ladder and form an obstacle course boot camp and charge $5 for 2 weeks and teach them how to run through tires and the rope ladder and use their arms to lift the ropes up and down (in a snakelike motion) to work out their upper bodies. Think outside the box on this one. If you are good at any type of fitness routine, and have knowledge that can be passed on to others, this is a quick, easy way to make some cash. Extra benefits of forming a club include building fitness-minded friendships with other like-minded people.

*WHAT OTHER SKILLS/TALENTS/HOBBIES CAN YOU TEACH FOR MONEY?

Just think how many people are out at restaurants and bars, wine tastings, scrapbook conventions, and quilting retreats. Think how many people buy books on how to get organized, how to start a home business, how to fix a computer, how to update and clean up your computer, how to begin and stick with a hobby. You get the idea. Do this yourself for money! Here's how.

If you are great at computers, post a service for a "personal computer clean up/update service." Friends and family can start dropping off their laptops for $10 and for that fee, you will clean up their computer, update their computer and perhaps audit the software to see if anything is outdated. Put flyers out, post your services on Craig's List, spread the word with family and friends, use Facebook or the community and college bulletin boards to put the word out. The process of updating or defragmenting a computer is very time consuming and many people go years without updating their computers. For just $10, this is a quick, easy way to make money. Plus it is cheap enough that it makes sense for other people to pay you to do this.

Host a wine tasting. People pay $75 for good wine tastings. So they certainly would come to your house and pay just $10 or $20 each. Have a theme wine tasting, such as bottles for $10 or under, or wines from different regions. Buy $50 worth of wine and if you charge each person $10, which is very cheap, and 25 people show up, that is $250 minus your $50 wine investment...so you've just make $200 in just one evening! Don't forget, it is a wine tasting, therefore, no one expects a "huge pour" and 1 bottle of wine can easily fit in 25 wine glasses if you pour a "tasting pour." This is a fun, easy way to mingle and to make significant extra cash. Plus, if each friend brings a friend, you've made new contacts for the following month, if you choose to do this once a month. Research the wines, where they are made and what the ingredients are, and make up flash cards for each wine sampled. Wine enthusiasts love to take notes, and this way, every guest can take their notes home. You can get creative with the flash cards and note sheets, making them attractive, and placing your contact information on the back side, much like a large business card. This is a very simple and cheap way to give an extra little something to your guests.

Couponers are the rage right now! I have personally come across seminars advertised where potential couponers pay $35 to learn how to coupon for an afternoon. If you are a great couponer, host a "coupon 101" night. Charge $5 and teach people how to organize themselves, how to begin couponing, what stores to shop at, what days are best to shop, etc. If you get 10 neighborhood women together for 2 hours, you have just made $50 bucks. Not bad at all! This goes for sweepstaking, internet freebies, mystery shopping, etc. If you are good at a certain hobby, or interest, and have a bit of knowledge and organizational skill, then you are qualified! Give your guests a printout with a list of websites, a "how to get started" printout, and background information. Guests will come to you to learn, and more importantly, they will pay you for your knowledge. As long as you keep it nominal, say $2 to $5, you will see that many, many guests will show up, as people love learning something new, and more importantly, they love learning something new with other people in a group setting!

Hobbies. Quilting, scrapbooking, embroidery, woodworking, furniture refinishing, stenciling, painting. All these hobbies require a little bit of expertise and if you have been working with the hobby for while, it may be worth it to help teach others. If you keep the cost low, most people would love to learn something new for nominal cost. Somewhere in the $2 to $5 range seems to be the most successful, in my experience. Who wouldn't love to learn a new technique or hobby for such a small amount of money each week? You can do this in your home and if you ask each guest to bring an appetizer or finger food, then you also have leftovers to eat for lunch the next day! Brilliant!

*WHAT SKILL CAN YOU SELL?

Everyone sets goals at the beginning of each year. Common goals are "I want to learn something new" or "I want to get back in shape." Remember what you read above regarding the fitness routines? This follows the same line of thought. The below suggestions are skills that you can teach others, if you have experience in the following sports. Of course, these are just suggestions and if you are good at any type of sport that is not listed here, just substitute it and follow the same guidelines. I have been most successful with this scenario: charge $5 or $10 for a 2-4 week course. This way you have a commitment for at least 2 to 4 weeks to build a relationship with your customers, making them more likely to return again and again. Make friends with parents of little kids who would pay another $5 or $10 for 4, half hour sessions to help their child be ready for that next game, or just to give their child an edge over the other teammates. If you have 5 kids attend at the same time, you just made $50 bucks (if you charge $10 per kid).

Some examples are as follows:

Soccer. Footwork or goalie skills.

Lacrosse. Goalie techniques, throwing and catching skills.

Tennis. Hitting, running, rules of the game.

Baseball. Catching, throwing, batting, stealing bases, and running.

Fishing. Bait a hook, cast, catch, filet, clean, cook.

Hockey. Goalie and shooting techniques.

Football. Throwing, catching, kicking, running.

Swim. Different strokes and techniques for breathing.

*WHAT EVERY-DAY-SERVICES CAN YOU OFFER?

Many people do not have time to perform their daily household chores. That's the bottom line. They are so busy with work, taking care of children and elderly parents, paying bills and basically running the rat race. Listen to your coworkers, friends and family and you will realize how many of them complain about how they do not have any time to pick up their dry-cleaning, run errands, grocery shop, etc. Cash in on this! Spread the word to family and friends that you will charge $2 to $5 to run errands, pick up prescriptions, select a birthday present and wrap it, or pick out a sympathy card and mail it. If you want to narrow it down and perform a specific household chore, then just focus on that one chore. I have listed some examples below. Show you are trustworthy, timely, and loyal, and you will quickly gain word-of-mouth customers.

Ironing. Buy cheap laundry baskets. Whatever fits inside the basket, you will iron for $20. So if you iron 5 family members' items (or friends' items), then you have just made $100. I, for one, would happily pay $20 to get my ironing all done! Experiment with the amount, but I have found that charging a very nominal fee, gets attention. Remember, you don't want to become independently wealthy ironing, you just want an extra couple hundred or thousand in cash over the course of 6-12 months, to buy the "extras" that you could not otherwise afford.

Cooking. Cook all day on a Sunday and have your friends and family members pick up what you have made in plastic containers for $5-$10 per meal. In other words, make a meal prep service. This may take some outlay of money, but if you spend $50 on ingredients and sell $100 worth of food, then you just made $50 in a few hours of cooking. This may take some calculating to see how much to charge to make it cost effective. Remember, pasta is cheap but meat is not, so definitely write out your calculations first. The last thing you want to do is go through all that effort and time, only to break even.

Pet sit/Dog walk. Put some flyers out to dog walk or pet sit. Pet owners pay big money to board their pets while they are away on vacation. Make some contacts, spread the word, and you can easily make $100 in one weekend of dog sitting or cat sitting.

Gardening/landscape/lawn mowing. Charge $5 per hour or even a flat fee of $20 to clean, rake, mow, weed a lawn. This may take a few hours, but if you do a few yards per weekend, you may very well make $60 dollars in cash, and, as an added bonus, you got your exercise in. Once one neighbor's yard looks spectacular, chances are the other neighbors will ask "who did your yard?" That is when you become very busy on the weekends and make a lot of extra cash! It happens quickly, so be ready for it.

Handyman. Everyone has little things to be done around their house. If you have a long ladder, offer to change light bulbs, hang ceiling fans, dust on top of plant shelves, etc. for a nominal fee. Either charge by the hour, or by the job. Say, $5 to change light bulbs, or flat fee of $20 to install a ceiling fan that may take you 20 minutes. Make sure you have the skills and be knowledgeable about electrical and plumbing issues before you try anything that involves those services. First and foremost, follow safety rules and double check electricity related items to be sure you follow all safety procedures. When in doubt, don't do it.

Pressure washing. Patios, sidewalks, and garage floors become moldy and downright disgusting over time. Many people do not have the time or stamina to make the effort to pressure wash these areas, because it is very messy to do. Yet, it looks so nice and clean afterwards. Offer to pressure wash these areas for your neighbors, friends and family, and over time, word of mouth will spread and you will have a nice little cash side business.

Hair/Makeup. If you are good at cutting hair, or applying make-up, try this as a side business. Men's haircuts are easy and generally take about 15 minutes of time, yet you can make $10 to $15 cash in that time frame. If you are exceptionally good at make-up, try to obtain word of mouth and when prom/homecoming time rolls around in your local community, you can make quick cash just from a few weekends. Young women do not have a lot of money to spend on professional make-up, so this can be a very good source of income, plus it is a lot of fun!

Organization. Offer to organize a closet, a garage, a home office, or a work shed for a nominal fee. There are unorganized people everywhere, and there are a lot of professional companies who organize a home for a very large amount of money. Why not you? Organize a filing cabinet and use a label maker. Your customer will be so much more productive once everything is organized, and they will be forever grateful.

Photographs. Who has time to organize photographs? If you are good at this somewhat tedious task, take advantage of those who do not have the time or patience to go through their old boxes of polaroids. Take it one step further. Offer to make a scrapbook or a power point presentation for upcoming birthdays, graduations, homecomings, anniversaries, corporate retreats and other special occasions. This is tedious and time consuming, but also fun, and a very good way to make extra cash quickly. You could also organize photos digitally on a computer or thumb drive. Pictures tend to get out of hand quickly and need to be organized immediately. Many people do not take the time to do this. If you are given a thumb drive full of pictures to organize, it is fairly easy to determine which pictures go where. For example you will obviously see birthday celebration pictures and then sporting event pictures. Just organize them into a logical folder and the owner of those pictures will be forever grateful for this service. This is a very tedious project and $10 or $20 for an entire afternoon is not great money, but again, you are not looking to get rich. You are looking for extra, fast cash!

Car wash/detail. It amazes me how many people pay to have their car washed and detailed. Do a great job with a small amount of friends and family and charge them either a flat rate or by the hour. You will quickly have regular customers and you could end up with extra monthly cash every single month.

Cleaning. One automatically thinks of cleaning other people's homes for extra money and this is certainly an opportunity especially in affluent neighborhoods. However, remember that entire office buildings, as well as individual law firms, doctors' offices and accountants, pay to have their offices cleaned, oftentimes after hours, so this is a perfect opportunity to make extra dough after your "day job." Make cheap business cards on the computer and place them on local business bulletin boards to advertise your cleaning services. If you do a good job, certainly word of mouth will get around and your side business may turn into a full time job over time.

*WHAT CAN YOU MAKE FROM SCRATCH?

As my kids' say, "in the olden days," farmer's wives made their own soap, grew their own herbs, and tended to their vegetable gardens. Why not give it a whirl? Find out (or maybe you already know) how to make candles, soaps and bottled perfumed water. This may take a little outlay of money, but think of who you can sell these homemade items to. Family and friends would buy these items, and would love to spread the word that their loved ones created something so special and out of the ordinary. Use social media to spread the word about the products you create. You can also give the items as gifts for birthdays, and other special occasions, thereby saving money. If you grow tomatoes and peppers and sell them for a third of the cost of what the grocery store sells them for, then neighbors, friends and family will no doubt buy them from you.

What about household cleaners? Most cleaning solutions are made from baking soda, vinegar, and other ingredients. Look on the internet to research how to make homemade cleaners, try them in your own home first, and if you get a good result, either put the ingredients in a bottle and sell it (with those glass jars you picked up during bulk pick up day or that garage sale). You can also hold a "Cleaning Party Night" and charge people $5 where you teach people how to make their own cleaners, what ingredients you use for each area of the house, and give them a printout of each cleaning "recipe" to bring home.

If you bring your homemade salsa to all the neighborhood parties and everyone raves about it, figure out the cost, then place a modest profit on top of it, jar it, and sell it. Do this for candies, chocolates, cookies, pies, etc.

*GET CRAFTY

Gather picture frames from around the house, garage sales, and look for them during your bulk pick up day adventure. Nail or glue the frames back together if they are broken, paint them vintage colors such as silver, gold and copper. Gather old black and white photographs from thrift shops, garage sales, online stock photo sites, or even your own attic and place them in the frames. You can also take pictures in black and white of your city's buildings, parks and waterways. Place those pictures in your new picture frames and sell them. People love vintage photographs, and black and white photos. Get creative with this idea and modify it any way you would like!

Go to old vintage shops and find hats. Then hot glue flowers and other items onto the hat, post pictures to your social media sites, and you will begin to receive comments. If you receive positive feedback, offer to make one for a friend for $10. You should also hunt for websites where you can upload your crafty items for free, and sell them online to the masses.

If you are a baker, take pictures of your cakes, pies and cookies and when someone you know has a birthday, baby shower, bridal shower, or other special occasion, offer to bake a cake. People spend $50 to $100 on some cakes!

Beautiful stationary, invitations, thank you notes and bridal/new baby announcements can easily and cheaply be created with rubber stamps, scrapbook paper, embellishments and stickers. Wrap a bundle with twine, decorate the envelopes to go with the paper products, and sell the bundles online or at a booth at a local flea market. Lovely letters and invitations are always a welcome sight in the mailbox amid all of the bills everyone receives.

Fashion jewelry is a very creative way to bring your personality to life, but also to make extra money on the side. Online craft sites, flea markets, local festivals, fresh markets are all potential spaces in which you can sell your jewelry. No matter what jewelry you design, surely there are many people who will enjoy wearing your creations. Men enjoy thicker bracelets and rings, while women enjoy everything from boho to elegant to holiday to industrial-looking. You can really get creative with earring and necklace sets for women or ring and bracelet sets for men. Remember that gemstones, beads, metals, crystals, seashells, rocks and other items you find for cheap can be implemented within your designs.

There are so many ways to make quick cash, not just a few dollars, but real money, if you just think outside the box a little bit. Think of what you are good at, what you are passionate about, what motivates you, and try to incorporate that into a cash business.

Start with friends and family and as word of mouth spreads, you may end up with a pretty sizable side business going on. All cash! You can be your own entrepreneur before long!

*OTHER IDEAS

Below are some other, more common, ideas for you to think about trying.

- Create an Ebook
- Create a web video or tutorial to show off your talent or skill
- Write a movie script
- Create a product or invention
- Look at products and decide how to make it better
- Create a patentable idea
- Write lyrics
- Create artwork or sculptures
- Write resumes, cover letters and business plans

Readers, I wish the best of luck to all of you! I sincerely hope you enjoyed my ideas. Remember, you can talk all day long about any idea or invention, but until you execute that idea, it is lost to the universe. Get a plan, and execute it! You can do this! You can make extra cash very quickly! My motto has always been "Why not me?" Chant this to yourself. You have to believe it can happen. Nothing comes without some sweat and some long hours, but I know you are up to the challenge. I would LOVE to hear from anyone who has put one of these ideas into motion and I would love to hear how it turned out. I love success stories!

If you have any questions at all, if you would like to comment, or if you have other great ideas of how to make quick, easy cash, please let me know!

Wishing You Many Blessings and Lots of Cash,

Caroline Fielding, at info@dryveninc.com

www.ingramcontent.com/pod-product-compliance
Lightning Source LLC
Chambersburg PA
CBHW071604170526
45166CB00004B/1795